A Practical Guide to
BUSINESS WRITING

Writing in English for non-native speakers

D0188025

Khaled Mohamed Al Maskari

WILEY

Contents

About the Author

Khaled Mohamed Al Maskari is an Emirati author based in Abu Dhabi, United Arab Emirates. With over 16 years of experience in the oil and gas industry, Al Maskari has held a number of leadership positions with governmental organizations in the United Arab Emirates in the field of Human Resources development and training. He has always been involved in assisting graduate students develop their business writing skills.

He won the Best Emirati Book Award 2011 for his book *A Practical Guide to Business Writing*, a helpful Business English guide for non-native speakers of English in the region. He has also been nominated Author of the Year 2011 by the Webpreneur Academy based in Dubai in recognition of his dedication and innovations in the fields of education and entrepreneurship.

He gained a Bachelor's degree in Electrical Engineering from Southern Illinois University, in the United States.

To learn more about Khaled's programs, you can go to his website www.khaledalmaskari.com or email Khaled on kalmaskari@yahoo.com.

Foreword

Exciting, informative, directional, and extremely helpful are just some of the words to describe *A Practical Guide to Business Writing*.

The content is clear and concise and, in a nutshell, it gives us some clear-cut guidelines to achieve a more accomplished communicative system in any organization.

This book can help you develop the qualities of an effective communicator, and no matter where you are on the administration ladder in your company, using the examples in this book will make whatever you write and wish to communicate more effective.

It is good – very good!

Dr. Clarence Emslie

Preface

This book contains a wealth of practical information for any person who aims to produce short effective documents within the work environment of the early 21st century.

It is not simply a guide to business writing. It does not focus on writing rituals, nor does it compare different uses of the English language for writing purposes. There is no in-depth attention to why our writing should have a certain tone, tendency or technique. There are many works in the market that accommodate such areas of business written English.

What this work offers are sensible, valuable and helpful rules for producing effective short reports, memos, letters and e-mails that are clear, concise and easy to read for the busy manager or supervisor working in the demanding setting of modern industry and commerce.

But it goes further: not only are rules offered to the inexperienced business writer, but models are proposed for various situations: apologizing, complaining, requesting, describing, recommending etc.

How do you:

- Open a document?
- Support your purpose?
- Address different readers?
- Close a document?

The solutions are here.
What are the most common errors people make in business writing and how can the writer cope with these inaccuracies?

The solutions are here.
What form should a written text take? Is there a format, model or template that can be utilized quickly and easily? Of course there is.

The solutions are here.
If your work requires you to produce short effective documents, then you are lucky to have this work on your desk. Read it. Enjoy it. Use it.

Michael Doherty

Introduction

Based on my experience in the field and my intention to assist and train fresh graduates, I conducted research which aimed at identifying techniques and tools to promote effective communication in writing. It was apparent that staff inability to write effective business letters or e-mails was their major impediment to effective communication in the workplace.

In fact, fresh graduates lack effective writing skills and may possess only moderate competence in the linguistic and rhetorical skills needed to produce appropriate, meaningful and accurate written documents in various genres. The intention to put together a set of basic principles that readers can use to write effectively was crucial.

The book, therefore, is designed for fresh graduates as well as other professionals who truly wish to develop overall proficiency in writing effective business letters and e-mails in order to communicate successfully and with integrity in the workplace.

As most correspondence takes place via e-mails nowadays, I focused heavily on this specific medium, which I consider to be a prominent communication tool in the business environment.

This book is locally produced and meant to address the most problematic aspects of business letter writing. It is a comprehensive guide that takes its readers through the whole process using straightforward language accessible to all. It also gives readers an in-depth overview of the major techniques, examples, graphical and contextual supports needed to enhance their writing abilities.

What Does
this Book Cover?

Chapter 1, Business Writing Style:
offers guidelines to different language aspects of business English, advising the writer to be directed by the purpose of the document, their relationship to the reader, and the content that satisfies the purpose and the reader.

Chapter 2, Business Memos:
examines the various parts of the business memo and its basic structure, offering a wide range of templates for the most common types of memo.

Chapter 3, Business E-mails:
considers the various parts of the e-mail, giving rules on what to do, what not to do, and showing the writer how to make use of Microsoft facilities.

Chapter 4, Common Writing Errors:
advises vigilance for common errors seen in the writing habits of others, showing how these can be detected and corrected.

Chapter 5, Useful Business Phrases:
scrutinizes the document function (i.e. the purpose of the report, memo, e-mail etc.), presenting several outlines for opening, developing and closing the document. Many samples for how to address the reasons for communication are provided.

Chapter 6, Confusing Words:
addresses the vocabulary frequently used in everyday writing tasks, highlighting those words most commonly misused, and giving contextual examples to help the writer appreciate the differences.

Chapter 7, Personal Business Documents:
offers a variety of samples for a range of typical business purposes, providing the business writer with practical business solutions.

Chapter 1
Business Writing Style

This chapter is intended to provide tips for effective business writing that can be applied to all forms of business correspondence such as: memos, faxes, reports, and e-mails.

Use these 12 tips to develop an effective business writing style:

1. Keep your purpose, readers and content in mind

2. Keep your sentences short

3. Use positive language

4. Use linking words

5. Use simple, familiar words

6. Use passive voice for specific reasons

7. Use bullet points and numbered lists correctly

8. Use tables and charts effectively

9. Use impersonal style when expressing opinions

10. Avoid outdated expressions

11. Avoid repetition

12. Avoid turning verbs into nouns

1. Keep your purpose, readers and content in mind

Before you start writing your e-mail, memo or report, consider the following points and keep in mind the PRC (Purpose, Reader, Content) Triangle (see fig 1.1 below).

? Purpose

What is my purpose?

- To inform
- To persuade
- To complain
- To appreciate

- To request
- To suggest or recommend
- To explain

↕ Readers

Who are my readers?

- Supervisors
- Trainees
- Managers
- Others

- Assistants
- Technicians
- Employees

🗐 Content

- What information do my readers want?
- Will my readers understand technical terms?
- Would examples, details, or graphics help the readers to understand better?

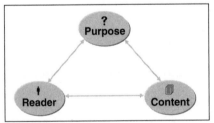

Figure 1.1   PRC Triangle

Remember

You should keep in mind the PRC Triangle when writing a memo, an e-mail or a report. This shows that the purpose, reader and content of a report are all equally important but that each is influenced by the others (see figure 1.1).

2. Keep your sentences short

In business writing, the fewer words, the better.

The following examples illustrate how to remove unnecessary words that do not add meaning to a sentence.

Long	Short
One of the best things you can do for yourself to improve your writing is to learn how to cut words that are not necessary. 25 words	To improve your writing, cut out unnecessary words. 8 words
Make your employees sufficiently aware of the potentially adverse consequences involved regarding these chemicals. 14 words	Warn your employees about these chemicals. 6 words
In view of the fact that the motor failed twice during the time that we tested it, we are at this point in time looking for other options. 28 words	Since the motor failed twice during testing, we are now looking at other options. 14 words
To be sure of obtaining optimal results, it is essential that you give your employees the resources that are necessary for completion of the job. 25 words	To get the best results, give your employees the resources they need to complete the job. 16 words
Our intention is to implement the verification of the reliability of the system in the near future. 17 words	We want to verify the system's reliability soon. 8 words

Long	Short
Let me know as to whether or not we can start drilling in view of the fact that the problem has not been fixed at the present time. 28 words	Since the problem has not yet been fixed, let me know whether we can start drilling. 16 words
We hereby advise you, as per your request, that we will be forwarding a copy of the contract to you in due course. 23 words	A copy of the contract will be sent to you in a few days as requested. 16 words
I will be unable to attend your May 6 meeting. I would like to say the reason is that I will be attending the leadership course in Dubai on the same day. 32 words	I will be unable to attend the May 6 meeting as I will be attending the leadership course in Dubai. 20 words
In this e-mail we have attempted to answer all of your questions and we hope that if you have any additional questions whatsoever, please do not hesitate to contact us immediately. 31 words	If you have any additional questions, please call us. 9 words

Remember

- Try to limit yourself to one idea per sentence.
- Break down longer sentences into simpler, shorter sentences.

3. Use positive language

In business writing it is important to use positive language in order to get the results you want.

As you can see in the examples below, the column on the right turns the negative words into positive words to obtain a positive reader response.

Negative	Positive
We are **unable** to promote you to supervisor because you **do not have** the skills and experience required for this position.	We will be able to promote you to supervisor when you meet the experience required for this position.
We **will not** start repairing your test equipment until we receive a deposit.	We will begin repairing your test equipment once we receive a deposit.
This is the second time that you **do not bother** to follow and stick to the duty roster.	This is to remind you again that your attendance is required.
If you **fail** to provide the specifications by the May 1 deadline, the project will **fail**.	By providing the specifications by May 1, you can be assured that the project will be on time.
You **cannot** reconnect without logging on again.	Log on again to reconnect.
The corporation **will not** pay unless employees also contribute.	The corporation will pay only if employees contribute.

Negative	Positive
You **neglected** to send us your passport copy and therefore we **cannot** process your request.	We will be able to process your request as soon as we receive a copy of your passport.
It is **bad not** to review the spare parts availability before submitting a work request.	It is good to review the spare parts availability before submitting a work request.
I hope that you **will not** be **disappointed** with the quality of our report.	I am sure that you will be delighted with the quality of our report.
The parts your company sent us the last time were the wrong size. Do **not** do this again.	We hope the parts will arrive as ordered.
We **cannot** send your order from our store until June 1, 2004.	Your order will be sent to you on June 1, 2004.
You failed to include your company number, so we **cannot** process your application.	We will be glad to process your application as soon as we receive your company number.
This problem **would not have** happened if you had connected the wires properly in the first place.	This problem may be resolved by connecting the wires as shown in the handbook.

Remember

- Write with a positive attitude by paying attention to the words and expression you choose to get the results you want.
- Sentences should be positive unless there is a reason to stress the "not," "no" or "never."

4. Use linking words

Linking words help establish clear connections between ideas and ensure that sentences and paragraphs flow together smoothly, making them easier to read.

The following table summarizes the most common group of linking words used in business writing:

Function	Signals	Examples
Addition	**And**	• Your salary adjustment has been reviewed **and** approved by the operations committee.
	In addition	• **In addition** to cleaning the valve, the entire machine was inspected.
	Also	• The parts are cheap and they are **also** well made.
	Moreover	• The supplier will deliver the unit. **Moreover**, he will supervise its installation on site.
	Furthermore	• You are requested to submit the drawing for the Gas Project. **Furthermore**, inform us of the starting date.

Function	Signals	Examples
Cause and Effect	**Because (of)**	• The flight was delayed **because of** fog.
	Due to	• Internet users had a hard time accessing the web **due to** the international hacking competition yesterday.
	Therefore	• The pay rate is not clearly defined. **Therefore**, it is recommended that the contract should not be signed yet.
	As a result	• The morale and overall capabilities of our trainees have shown a remarkable improvement **as a result** of your efforts.
	Consequently	• The spare parts did not arrive on time. **Consequently**, I contacted the suppliers.
	Hence	• The number of trainees has been increased. **Hence**, we should monitor their attendance and performance.

Function	Signals	Examples
Contrast	But	• The software is expensive, **but** it meets our requirements.
	However	• The meeting scheduled for Monday was cancelled. **However**, we will meet sometime next week.
	Yet	• This is acceptable, **yet** it could be better.
	Although	• **Although** no complaints have been received, we think that the use of the internet must now be monitored.
Purpose	In order to	• We are writing to you **in order to** clarify certain confusing points.
	So that	• The new employees must be trained in a practical hands-on manner **so that** we can bring their performance up to acceptable levels.
	So	• Our office printer is running low on ink, **so** please refrain from printing unimportant documents for the time being.

Function	Signals	Examples
Concession	**Despite**	• **Despite** being issued a warning letter, your attendance record has not improved.
	In spite of	• **In spite of** previous memos, private car owners are still parking their cars in the administration building areas.
Alternatives	**Either . . . or . . .**	• We plan **either** to adjust your salary **or** to promote you to operations supervisor.
	Neither . . . nor . . .	• We have **neither** the spare parts **nor** the manpower to carry out this task.
	Or	• Do you need to receive your order in one day **or** in three days?

5. Use simple, familiar words

We write to express, not to use every word in the dictionary. Avoid using big words to convey your meaning clearly. For example, instead of "magnitude and configuration," say "size and shape."

Always try to use the simplest word possible.

Big word	Simple word
accrue	add, gain
acquire	get, buy
alleviate	reduce
allocate	assign
ameliorate	improve
anticipate	expect, await
apparent	clear
apprise	tell
articulate	explain
ascertain	find out
attain	reach, meet, achieve
attributable	due to
caveat	warning
cease	stop, end

Big word	Simple word
cogitate	think
cognizant of	aware of
commensurate	equal
concur	agree
confront	face
consolidate	combine, join
consummate	complete or finish
contemplate	consider
convene	meet
deem	consider
designate	appoint
detrimental	harmful
dispatch	send
disseminate	give, issue, pass, send
encounter	meet
enumerate	list
facilitate	make easier, help

Big word	Simple word
furnish	send, give
inception	start
incombustible	fireproof
initiate	start
interrogate	question
manifest	clear, obvious
mitigate	reduce
numerous	many
obviate	avoid
peruse	review
possess	own
preclude	prevent
promulgate	issue, publish
ratify	approve, confirm
recapitulate	sum up

Big word	Simple word
reimburse	pay back
reiterate	repeat
remunerate	pay
render	give, make
retain	keep
reveal	show
scrutinize	inspect
solicit	ask for, request
strategize	plan
streamline	update, simplify
transpire	take place, occur
utilize	use

As you write, remember that the goal of business writing is to communicate with your readers, not to impress them with your vocabulary.

Below are good examples of simple words to be used rather than difficult ones in order to convey your message clearly to your readers.

Unclear	Clear
He **discerned** that the **promulgated** policy would work.	He **knew** the **proposed** policy would work.
As **stipulated**, we **extrapolated** the budget figures for two years.	As **required**, we **estimated** the budget figures for two years.
Will you **utilize** instruction manuals during the **obligatory** training period?	Will you **use** instruction manuals during the **required** training period?
We **anticipate** that most of the options will be **fundamental** enough to meet our needs.	We **expect** that most of the options will be **basic** enough to meet our needs.
Remember to **incorporate** all the other good writing principles you have learned in this course.	Remember to **include** all the other good writing principles you have learned in this course.

Remember

Avoid using difficult words when simple words will communicate your message.

6. Use the passive voice for specific reasons

The choice between using active or passive voice in business writing is a matter of style. Most books recommend using active voice. However, there is an exception to this rule.

Sometimes passive voice can be useful in an effort to sound more diplomatic and when you do not want to highlight the subject of the sentence.

When to use the passive voice?
The passive voice is to be preferred in the following cases:

1. Use the passive voice when you do not want to identify who performed the action.

 Examples:

- Smoking is prohibited.
- A new safety policy was introduced after the accident.
- The new offices were decorated last week.
- The error has been corrected.
- The centrifugal pump was installed on May 12, 20xx.
- Procedures have been written to ensure safety.

2. Use the passive voice to describe a mistake to avoid blaming anyone in particular.

 Examples:

- Profits are down by 2%.
- The incident rate in ABC Field is increasing dramatically this year compared to last year.
- Computer sales dropped by 10 % during the summer.
- The monthly report was submitted late.

3. Use the passive voice when you don't know who carried out the action.

 Examples:

- Three computers were stolen from the training center.
- The training room was left unlocked.
- The briefcase was stolen at the airport terminal.
- The photocopier is broken.

Since people have little time to read, set out important points in a numbered or bulleted list. This makes it easier to scan so your readers get the meaning without reading every word.

When to use bulleted and numbered lists

Use numbered lists when working with instructions that are to be carried out in sequence. If the sequence of items is not essential, use bullets.

Example 1: Using bulleted lists

We are still having problems with the five new computers we have purchased from XYZ Computer Company. The problems we have been having include:

- Two notebook computers won't boot up.
- One monitor continues to make a high-pitched, whining sound.
- Two desktop computers became infected with viruses.

Example 2: Using bulleted lists

I raised your difficulty about arriving for work on time. I pointed out that:

- your managers had done their best to take account of your travel problems; and
- you had agreed with them that Dubai was the most convenient place for you to work.

However, your initial improvement was short-lived. Over the past two months your punctuality has dropped to a totally unacceptable level.

By using bulleted lists, you draw your reader's attention to important items.

Example 3: Using numbered lists

To: Amar Jones
From: Khaled Mohamed
Date: March 5. 20xx
Subject: Procedure for Handling Payroll Advances

There is a new procedure (to reflect updated policies) for obtaining payroll advances. Our employees will find it an improvement on the old confusing procedure. The new procedure is as follows:

1. Obtain form for Payroll Advance from your supervisor.
2. Complete the form by filling in all the blanks in the Employee Section form.
3. Get approval from your immediate supervisor.
4. Pick up your check from the cashier's office.

Example 4: Using numbered lists

To: All Employees Using XP 2000 Computers
From: Head of Information Technology
Date: March 5, 20xx
Subject: Computer Security Problem

Your cooperation is urgently needed to solve a serious computer security problem. To enable you to keep your files and those of the entire company secure, please follow these two actions:

1. Keep your password private and do not share it with anyone.
2. Log on to the computer manually.

Your adherence to the above is much appreciated.

By using numbers, you are directing your reader to carry out instructions in sequence.

Put lists of items in parallel form

Use parallel form to improve the clarity of your writing. To make your writing parallel, use the same grammatical form for all items in a list. In other words, match nouns with nouns, verbs with verbs, and phrases with phrases.

 Example: Parallel form in lists

Here are two versions of a passage. The first ignores the guidelines; the second follows them.

Weak List	Improved List
I left my job for several reasons: • Long hours • Poor pay • I found the work tedious • Equipment was dangerous	I left my job for several reasons: • Long hours • Poor pay • Tedious work • Dangerous equipment
The following preliminary work is required before work-over: 1. Remove pen-fold fence. 2. Removing crash barrier. 3. Clear cellar of sand. 4. Remove safety valve. 5. Master valves need to be checked for leakage.	The following preliminary work is required before work-over: 1. Remove pen-fold fence. 2. Remove crash barrier. 3. Clear cellar of sand. 4. Remove safety valve. 5. Check master valves for leakage.

Remember

- If the sequence matters, use a **numbered** list.
- If the order does not matter, use a **bulleted** list.
- Use parallel form to achieve balanced writing.

8. Use tables and charts effectively

Tables, charts and other graphs are quick, effective ways for your reader to get information. People don't always read everything in a report, but they often look at the visuals.

In this section, we will concentrate on when to use tables and charts effectively to enhance your written presentation and to draw your readers' attention.

Tables

Use a table to present data and facts to improve clarity.

 Example:

Department	Current Month	Year to Date
Drilling	$ 2,000	$ 5,000
Inspection	$ 1,200	$ 4,300
Operations	$ 3,300	$ 10,000
Safety	$ 1,200	$ 2,500
Technical	$ 3,000	$ 5,200
Total	**$ 10,700**	**$ 27,000**

Table 1.1   Overtime expenses for all departments

The following charts are commonly used in technical reports:
- Line chart   • Pie chart   • Bar chart   • Flow chart

Line chart

Use a line chart to show trend data over extended time periods.

Example of line chart

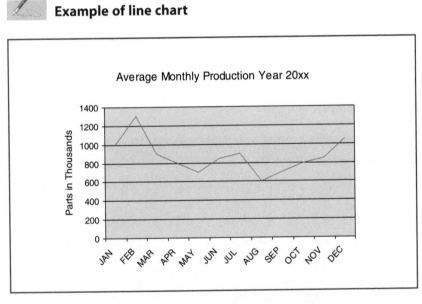

Figure 1.2   Line chart

Use a pie chart to show percentage or distribution of a whole.

Example of pie chart

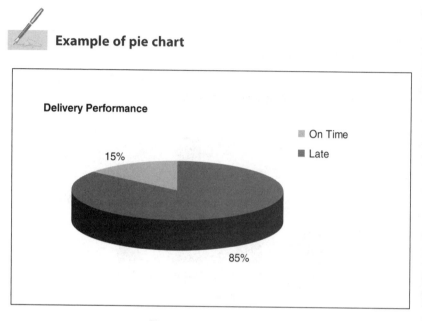

Figure 1.3   Pie chart

Use a bar chart to compare items with one another.

Example of bar chart

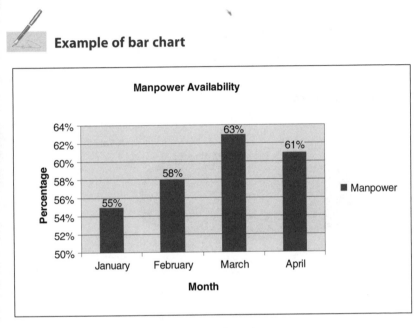

Figure 1.4   Bar chart

Flow chart

Use a flow chart to show a series of steps from beginning to end (e.g. procedure or process).

Flow chart symbols

Name	Symbol	Meaning
Oval		Start or end of the task
Rectangular		Steps
Diamond		Decisions
Flow line		Used to connect symbols and indicate the flow of logic

Example of flow chart

Figure 1.5 shows the major steps in the procedure for issuing a high voltage electrical certificate using flow chart symbols.

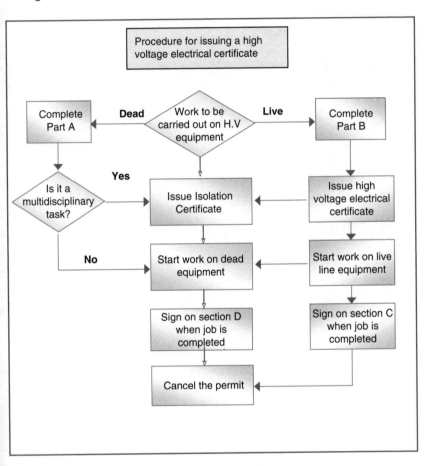

Figure 1.5   Flow chart

9. Use impersonal style when expressing opinions

Expressions like "I think" or "I feel" are rarely used in business reports because they are too personal. Managers are not looking for your personal opinion and feeling; they are looking for professional opinions.

Personal Style	Impersonal Style
I believe a bonus for our employees should be based on employees' performance.	The bonus for our employees should be based on employees' performance.
I expect that the use of computers will make it easier to compile our monthly production report.	The use of computers will make it easier to compile our monthly production report.
I feel certain that the new plan is better than the old method.	The new plan is better than the old method for the following reasons:
I think that by taking this course, it will help improve my writing skills. I know that I will learn how to use skills that are good to know in any job.	This course should improve my writing skills, teaching me skills that are good to know in any job.
I would like to recommend that everyone wear safety boots in the Power Station.	It is recommended that everyone wear safety boots in the Power Station.

10. Avoid outdated expressions

Here are some classic examples of outdated expressions to be avoided in business writing. Use modern language instead which is shorter and clearer.

Instead of this . . .	Try this . . .
Please send your comments not later than (date).	Please send your comments by (date).
Please find attached herewith . . .	Attached is . . .
Enclosed please find . . .	Enclosed is . . . or I have enclosed . . .
Please feel free to contact the undersigned on . . .	Please call me on . . .
As per your request . . .	As requested . . .
In accordance with your request . . .	As you requested . . .
We are hereby acknowledging receipt of your order . . .	We received your order . . .
Please be good enough to advise me . . .	Please let me know . . .
I would be glad if you could advise me when . . .	Please let me know when . . . .
Pursuant to your e-mail . . .	According to your e-mail . . .
I am writing this e-mail to convey my warmest congratulations on your promotion to . . .	Congratulations on your promotion to . . .

Instead of this . . .	Try this . . .
Thanking you in advance . . .	I appreciate your . . .
Please give your attention to the contents of enclosed brochures.	Please see the enclosed brochures.
I would be very happy if it would be possible to send me . . .	Please send me . . .
It may be of some concern to you to learn that your pump is ready for testing.	Your pump is ready for testing.
Your attention is directed to the contents of enclosed brochures.	Please see the enclosed brochures.
Thanking you in advance for cooperation in this matter.	Thank you for your cooperation in this matter.
Pursuant to your request, two contracts are attached hereto.	As you requested, two contracts are attached.
Should you require any further clarification please do not hesitate to contact the undersigned.	Please call me if you have any questions.
Please furnish details.	Please send me details.

Instead of this . . .	Try this . . .
I regret to inform . . .	I am sorry . . .
Permit me to say	(never use)
Let me take this opportunity	(never use)
As of this date in time	Now
In light of the fact that...	Because or Since
In view of the fact that	Because or Since
In the event that	If
Per diem	Daily

Remember

Try to write in similar fashion to the way you speak in a business meeting. The clarity of your writing will improve and you won't sound boring.

11. Avoid repetition

Repetition means saying the same thing twice. The following examples indicate that it is a good idea to edit your writing to look for repetition and redundant words.

Repetition	Without Repetition
I think **the reason why** Lucas has been promoted to operations manager is **because** of his performance.	Lucas has been promoted to operations manager **because** of his performance.
We do not have the manpower to **carry out the major overhaul of the gas turbine** or the spare parts to **carry out the major overhaul of the gas turbine**.	We have neither the manpower nor the spare parts to **carry out the major overhaul of the gas turbine**.
I ask **the question whether** trainees can attend the gas turbine course.	I ask **whether** trainees can attend the gas turbine course.
Each **individual operator** will receive a bonus for completing the task on time.	Each **operator** will receive a bonus for completing the task on time.
Our Human Resources department is **planning in advance** a meeting to review the effectiveness of the new appraisal system.	Our Human Resources department is **planning** a meeting to review the effectiveness of the new appraisal system.
The August 8 meeting has been **postponed to a later date**.	The August 8 meeting has been **postponed**.

12. Avoid turning verbs into nouns

Using the noun form of the verb takes more words than using a strong verb. For example, instead of saying "make a decision" it is more effective to say "decide."

Noun Form	Verb Form
give instructions to	instruct
make a classification	classify
carry out an investigation of	investigate
perform an assessment	assess
make an observation	observe
conduct a review of	review
make adjustments	adjust

In the following examples, notice how much more straightforward and easy to understand the sentences are when presented with a strong verb form.

Examples

Instead of	Use this
The police **conducted an investigation** into the matter.	The police **investigated** the matter.
Our **intention** is to **perform an audit** of the records of the program.	We **intend** to **audit** the program.
My boss **has an expectation** that I will attend the Power and Gas Exhibition.	My boss **expects** me to attend the Power and Gas Exhibition.
Authorization was given by the Planning manager to purchase new computers.	The Planning manager **authorized** the purchase of new computers.
We hope you're willing to **undertake serious reconsideration** of your position.	We hope you will **reconsider** your position.
The function of this handout is the **improvement** of wordy writing.	This handout **improves** wordy writing.
The committee **made the decision** to reward all employees in the Production section.	The committee **decided** to reward all employees in the Production section.
The **implementation of** the plan was successful.	The plan was **implemented** successfully.
Take into consideration the cost of maintaining the data.	**Consider** the cost of maintaining the data.

Remember   Rely on the **verb** to do the work.

Summary

These tips provide the basics of good business writing and will always keep your written communications sharp and effective.

To produce effective documents, please use these tips every time you write.

1. Keep your purpose, readers and content in mind

2. Keep your sentences short

3. Use positive language

4. Use linking words

5. Use simple, familiar words

6. Use the passive voice for specific reasons

7. Use bullet points and numbered lists correctly

8. Use tables and charts effectively

9. Use impersonal style when expressing opinions

10. Avoid outdated expressions

11. Avoid repetition

12. Avoid turning verbs into nouns

Chapter 2
Business Memos

This chapter will assist you in preparing and writing memos that allow you to communicate effectively in today's workplace.

The first section explains the basic structure of a memo. The second section offers examples of the most common types of business memos. It concludes by giving you a checklist to keep in mind when writing memos.

Definition of a Memo
A memo is a document typically used for communication within a company.

The Basic Structure of a Memo

1. Heading

2. Purpose

3. Body

4. Conclusion

5. Closing

6. Carbon Copy "CC"

The basic structure of a memo is discussed in the following pages and illustrated in Figure 2.1 in section 6.

1. Heading

The heading section follows this general format:

To: readers' names or job titles
From: your name or job title
Date: current date is always included (e.g., February 6, 20xx)
Subject: what the memo is about (be specific)

Remember

Different companies may use other heading formats than the one which appears here; use whichever format your company prefers.

2. Purpose

The purpose section provides a brief statement to direct your reader to the purpose of your memo.

Example:

- We refer to your memo dated May 23, 20xx regarding the organization's update.
- Attached, as requested, is an updated training record for our trainees.
- It has been noticed that some employees are still smoking in the main office.
- All supervisors will meet June 3, 20xx at 10:00 a.m. to work out the annual operating budgets for all departments.

3. Body

The body section explains your request or response. It provides additional details to support the purpose statement.

 Example:

To: Human Resources Manager
From: Head of Employee Relations
Date: September 5, 20xx
Subject: New Employees

Two new employees have been hired to work in the Human Resources Department. Lila Hamdi will begin work on October 1, and Yassin Ali will begin on October 15.

Ms. Lila has worked for three years as an administrative assistant for another company. Due to her previous experience, she was hired as a Program Assistant.

Body

Mr. Yassin has just completed a one-year training program at Gulf Community College. He was hired as an Administrative Assistant.

I would like to introduce you to the new employees. Please schedule a time for a short visit.

4. Conclusion

The conclusion section reiterates the goal of the memo, and states any action required.

Examples:

- Your feedback on the attached proposal by May 10 would be appreciated.
- Please contact me if you require further information.
- Your cooperation in this regard is appreciated.
- I would appreciate your comments on this matter by March 20, xx.
- I look forward to receiving your approval on this matter.

5. Closing

The most common closings are:
- Sincerely,
- Yours sincerely,
- Regards,

6. Carbon copy "CC"

If your memo needs to be distributed, then list those people who should have a copy for their information only under "cc", but do not expect them to take any action.

	Memorandum
1 Heading	To: readers' names or job titles From: your name or job title Date: current date Subject: what the memo is about (be specific)
2 Purpose	In paragraph one, state the point or main idea of your memo.
3 Body	In paragraph two, provide the explanation and background data to support your point if required.
4 Conclusion	In paragraph three, conclude your memo with an action statement by telling your readers exactly what you want them to do.
5 Closing	Regards, Name Job Title
6 Carbon Copy	CC:

Figure 2.1   The basic structure of a memo

Example

Memorandum

1 Heading	To: Operation Supervisor From: Transport Supervisor Date: May1, 2003 Subject: Renewal of Driver's License
2 Purpose	Our records indicate that your driver's license will expire on July 30, 20xx.
3 Body	Please submit the following documents before May 15, 20xx in order to complete the processing formalities: • Three sets of clear passport photocopies • Two recent passport size photographs.
4 Conclusion	Your cooperation in this regard would be appreciated.
5 Closing	Regards, Amar Ahmed Transport Supervisor
6 Carbon Copy	CC: Head of Transport

Common types of memos

Memos are frequently used:

1. To inform

To provide information without necessarily expecting any action on the part of your readers.

 Example:

> To: Head of Department
> From: Mechanical Engineer
> Date: March 5, 20xx
> Subject: Absence from duty
>
> This is to inform you that I was unable to report for work on Tuesday and Wednesday of last week due to an illness that kept me confined to bed.
>
> A medical certificate from the hospital is attached for your files.
> Regards,
>
> Khalid Ali
> Mechanical Engineer

2. To request

To obtain permission, information, approval, help, or assistance.

Example:

> To: Head of Maintenance
> From: Senior Mechanical Engineer
> Date: September 15, 20xx
> Subject: Maintenance Management course
>
> I am interested in attending the above mentioned course, which will be held at the Hilton Hotel in Dubai from December 8–12, 20xx.
>
> This course will certainly enhance my knowledge of the subject and help me meet the maintenance challenges of our department.
>
> Your approval would be greatly appreciated.
> Regards,
>
> Lila Hamad
> Senior Mechanical Engineer

3. To instruct

To give information in the form of directions, instructions, or procedures.

 Example:

> To: All Employees
> From: ABC Plant Manager
> Date: April 16, 20xx
> Subjec: Private Vehicles
>
> In order to minimize road traffic accidents, employees bringing private vehicles to ABC plants are requested to adhere to the following regulations:
>
> 1. All private vehicles should be parked inside the accommodation complex.
> 2. Company transportation must be used for any work within the plant.
>
> Your strict adherence to the above will be much appreciated.
> Regards,
>
> Jassim Hansen
> ABC Plant Manager

4. To recommend

Suggesting an action or series of actions based on alternative possibilities that have been evaluated.

 **Example:**

To: Head of Safety
From: Senior Safety Engineer
Date: March 5, 20xx
Subject: Reverse Parking Sensor

It has been noticed that the number of accidents being reported as a result of reverse parking has increased in the past three months.

Therefore, it is recommended that sensors be installed on company vehicles to prevent further accidents.
Regards,

Hala Ali
Senior Safety Engineer

5. To respond

To act in response to your superior's questions about something related to your work. Also, you may respond to a previous communication.

 Example 1

> To: All Employees
> From: Human Resources Manager
> Date: March 5, 20xx
> Subject: Smoking Policy
>
> In response to many suggestions by employees throughout the company, we have developed a company policy that permits smoking only in **designated smoking rooms**.
>
> This policy applies to both employees and visitors to our office. If you have any questions please contact Ali in personnel services on extension 22555.
>
> Regards,
> Khaled Hamdi
> Human Resources Manager

 Example 2

> To: Mechanical Supervisor
> From: Team Leader
> Date: March 5, 20xx
> Subject: Business Writing Course
>
> In reply to your memo dated March 10, 20xx regarding the abovementioned subject, I am glad to inform you that your request has been approved.
>
> Please contact the training coordinator to make the necessary arrangement.
>
> Regards,
> Amar Jassim
> Team Leader

To express disapproval of an unsatisfactory situation.

Example

To:	Technical Support Manager
From:	Head of Maintenance
Date:	June 10, 20xx
Subject:	Compressor Failure

We are having frequent failures with the two valves installed recently in our gas facility. The problem has caused a severe decline in our production rate.

I would appreciate having someone from your company come and take an in-depth look at this problem.

Please let me know if you need more information.
Regards,

Mohamed Hansen
Head of Maintenance

To remind your employees about things which have to be completed or that have not been followed up appropriately.

Example

To:	All Employees
From:	Head of Planning
Date:	July 10, 20xx
Subject:	Use of copier

It has been noticed that some employees in this department are using copiers for other than company business.

All employees are therefore requested to limit the use of copies to company business only.

Your cooperation in this matter is appreciated.

Lila Ali
Head of Planning

8. To show appreciation

To show appreciation and gratitude for a job particularly well done.

Example 1

To:	Team Leader Power
From:	Plant Manager
Date:	July 15, 20xx
Subject:	Letter of appreciation

I am pleased to convey the management's appreciation for your active role and prompt response in getting our operations back to normal.

You have displayed valuable professional skills and dedication to your duties which are particularly noteworthy.

We rely upon your continued support in any such future emergencies.

Adel Hassan
Plant Manager

Example 2

To:	Team Leader Power
From:	Plant Manager
Date:	July 15, 20xx
Subject:	Letter of appreciation

We are pleased to inform you that you have been selected "Safety Employee of the Month" for raising your concerns about water coolers at ABC restaurants and suggesting a safe method.

Please accept a gift together with this letter as a token of the Management's appreciation.

Adel Hassan
Plant Manager

Remember the following top ten points when you write memos:

1. Use the proper memorandum format that your company prefers.

2. Use a specific subject line that summarizes the memo clearly.

3. Use short, simple sentences.

4. Focus each paragraph on one idea related to the subject.

5. Check spelling when the document is complete.

6. Identify yourself clearly.

7. Think of your reader.

8. Write it all on one page.

9. Keep it simple.

10. Keep a copy of all correspondence for future reference.

Chapter 3
Business E-mails

Today, it seems everyone is using e-mail for business communication. It is a quick, easy, flexible and fast method of communication.

In this chapter you will learn about e-mail techniques that are aimed at helping you communicate more effectively in the workplace.

Effective e-mail techniques

1. Write a clear subject line

2. Use the "cc" button

3. Use Out of Office Assistance

4. Use attachments for long documents

5. Keep your message short and to the point

6. Don't use e-mail for immediate action

7. Use the spell check

8. Use courteous language

9. Provide an action statement when necessary

10. Identify yourself clearly

11. Don't overuse abbreviations

12. Don't use all capitals when typing

1. Write a clear subject line

Write the subject lines clearly to let the recipient know what the message is about. What you write in the subject lines should reflect the content of the e-mail.

See the examples below on clear and unclear subject lines.

 Example 1

Subject: Seminar (**Not Clear**)
Subject: Security Management Seminar held by Siemens (**Clear**)

 Example 2

Subject: Photocopy Machine (**Not Clear**)
Subject: Authorization for Photocopy Machine Purchase (**Clear**)

Example 3

Subject: Information (**Not Clear**)
Subject: Request for Salary Information (**Clear**)

Example 4

Subject: Budget (**Not Clear**)
Subject: Quarterly Budget Review (**Clear**)

Example 5

Subject: Meeting (**Not Clear**)
Subject: Monthly Safety Meeting (**Clear**)

Example 6

Subject: Complaints (**Not Clear**)
Subject: Complaints about Cigarette Smoking in the Cafeteria
         (**Clear**)

2. Use the "cc" button

Use the "cc:" button for those individuals who need the information, but who would not be required to reply to your e-mail or take any action.

Example

From:	jassim@climaxtech.com
To:	ali@climaxtech.com
CC:	hassan@climaxtech.com; lila@climaxtech.com
Subject:	Safety Training Modules Presentation

Ali,

Please be prepared to make a ten-minute presentation on "Safety Training Modules" to all employees on June 15, 20xx, at 10.a.m. in the conference room.

Regards,

Jassim Mohammed
Safety Manager

In this e-mail Mr. Jassim requests Ali to deliver a presentation and he sends copies to Hassan and Lila for their information only.

Remember

- "**To**" is expected to respond.
- "**CC**" is expected to read the message as information only.

3. Use the Out of Office Assistant

The Out of Office Assistant automatically replies to email messages sent to you during your absence. By using this tool you can acknowledge receipt of the message, and advise the sender when you will be back at work and able to respond to their messages.

How to use the Out of Office Assistant
You can use this method from any computer that runs Microsoft Outlook.

1. Click on the **Tools** menu.
2. Select **Out of Office Assistant**.
3. Click on **I am currently out of the office** and enter a suitable message to be sent in your absence.
4. Click on **OK** to save the settings.
5. Repeat these steps and click **I am currently in the office** when you return.

Example:

From: jassim@climaxtech.com
To: khalid@climaxtech.com
Subject: Out of the Office Auto Reply

I will be out of the office from March 10 to15, attending the Gas Turbine conference.

Please contact Ali during the abovementioned period.

Jassim Hammed
Operations Supervisor

Use this feature when you are out of the office for a few days or when you are on leave.

4. Use attachments for long documents

Since not all computers have the same type of software, you should inform readers which program or software is needed to open your attachment.

It is best to inform your readers of the format of any **attachments** you send if they're anything other than basic Microsoft Office file types.

 Example:

To:	Mike@climaxtech.com
CC:	Ahmad@climaxtech.com
Subject:	ABC Company Profile
Attachment:	ABC Company Profile. PDF (90K)

Dear Mike,

Please find attached ABC® Company Profile.
Should you have any questions, please contact me on my mobile: 050/4434660.

Note: You require Acrobat Reader to open the attachment.

Regards,

Adel Ahmed
Consultant

Remember

- Before sending an attachment, consider whether your reader has the software to open and view the file.
- Be careful of file sizes; use zip files for extra large attachments.

5. Keep your message short

E-mail is meant to be brief. Keep your message short and to the point. Use only a few paragraphs and a few sentences per paragraph. (For further information, see Chapter 1, section 2.)

6. Don't use e-mail for immediate action

Don't use e-mail if you need an immediate reply or action. Remember that the person you are sending e-mail to may be in a meeting, out of office, or taking leave or absent. For any of these reasons, they may not be able to reply to you immediately.

For immediate responses use another, more personally direct means of communication such as mobile or telephone.

Remember

E-mail is a great way to quickly get information to many people, but may not be the right answer for all communications.

7. Use spell check

Some employees do not check their spelling before sending an e-mail. It only takes a few seconds to run a spell-check to pick up any spelling errors. This may influence whether your message is read, ignored or responded to.

Frequently misspelled business words

absence	accommodate
approximately	attendance
behavior	colleague
committee	competent
decision	develop
dilemma	discipline
efficiency	environment
existence	familiar
guarantee	guidance
immediately	maintenance
maneuver	millennium
relevant	technique

Remember

Make sure all words are spelled correctly. Spell check will not pick up words that are spelled correctly, but are misused within the context of the sentence. For example:

Wrong: You may wish to comment on <u>weather</u> the proposed plan meets your requirements.

Right: You may wish to comment on <u>whether</u> the proposed plan meets your requirements.

8. Use courteous language

Read the e-mail below and consider how you would feel if you were the reader. Then compare it with the revised e-mail which is written in a polite way.

Example

Original

	From:	jassim@climaxtech.com
	To:	ali@climaxtech.com
	Subject:	Work Permit

No greeting

Impolite message

I am no longer responsible for dealing with work permits so do not allow your staff to bring these permits to my office anymore.

Let your staff contact Hassan from now on for all permit matters.

No closing

Revised

	From:	jassim@climaxtech.com
	To:	ali@climaxtech.com
	Subject:	Work Permit

Appropriate greeting

Dear Ali,

Positive message

I have just transferred to the Training department. Please inform your staff to deal with Hassan from now on.
Your co-operation is appreciated.

Appropriate closing

Regards,
Jassim Hamad
Training Coordinator

9. Provide an action statement when necessary

At the end of your e-mail you should conclude with an action statement. What specifically, do you want your readers to do as a result of reading your e-mail?

Do you want them to reply to your e-mail, or is it for their information only?

Example

To: All employees
CC:
Subject: Virus–Caution

We have identified a virus in the form of an attachment with the word "Love", which will try to run itself, without the knowledge of your friends, partners or vendors.

Therefore, do not open any e-mail or save any attachment having the word "Love," even if it is from your trusted friends, partners, or vendors.

Action Statement

Regards,

Ali Salem
Information System Manager

10. Identify yourself clearly

When contacting someone outside your organization, always include your name, occupation title, contact number and any other contact information. This will help your reader to respond to you better.

Example

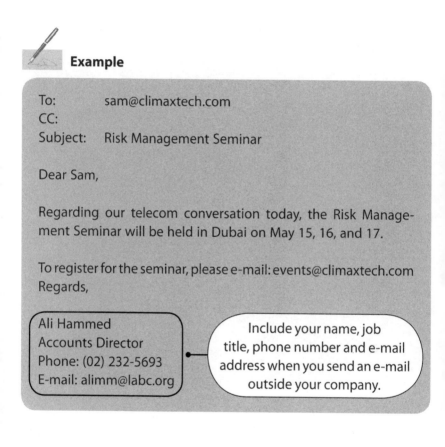

To: sam@climaxtech.com
CC:
Subject: Risk Management Seminar

Dear Sam,

Regarding our telecom conversation today, the Risk Management Seminar will be held in Dubai on May 15, 16, and 17.

To register for the seminar, please e-mail: events@climaxtech.com
Regards,

Ali Hammed
Accounts Director
Phone: (02) 232-5693
E-mail: alimm@labc.org

Include your name, job title, phone number and e-mail address when you send an e-mail outside your company.

Imagine you receive the following message, which uses many abbreviations.

 Example:

To: hassan@climaxtech.com
CC: lila@climaxtech.com
Subject: Risk Management Seminar
Attachment:

Ali,

Plz be informed that **u** are nominated **2** attend the Risk Management seminar which will be held **@** Hilton Hotel in Dubai from May 15-20, 20xx.

Let me know if **u** need more **info**.
Regards,

Ahmed Mohamed
Training Coordinator

The sender of this message uses many abbreviations such as **Plz** instead of please, **U** instead of you, **2** instead of to, **@** instead of at and **info** instead of information.

These abbreviations are acceptable in messages to close, personal friends, but are not appropriate in business e-mails. They often make the readers frustrated when trying to read your messages.

12. Do not use all capitals when typing

The original e-mail presented below is difficult to read and gives the reader the impression that they are being shouted at. Use capital letters to highlight an important word, but don't type your e-mail entirely in capital letters.

 **Example:**

Original

From:
To:
Subject: Employee of the Month Program

DEAR ALI,

STARTING IN OCTOBER WE WILL BEGIN RECOGNIZING A DIFFER-ENT EMPLOYEE FROM EACH DIVISION AS EMPLOYEE OF THE MONTH. SELECTION WILL BE MADE BY DIVISION MANAGERS AND WILL BE BASED ON THE FOLLOWING CRITERIA:

• PERFORMANCE OF DUTIES
• ATTENDANCE
• ATTITUDE

From:
To:
Subject: Employee of the Month Program

Dear Ali,

Starting in October we will begin recognizing a different employee from each division as Employee of the Month. Selection will be made by division managers and will be based on the following criteria:

- Performance of duties
- Attendance
- Attitude

Wouldn't you rather receive the revised version?

In order for business e-mails to be effective, please consider the top ten tips before you hit the Send button:

1. Keep your message short.

2. Make your subject line mean something.

3. Start your e-mail with Dear and end with a simple closing (Thanks or Regards).

4. Always spell words correctly!

5. Write in a positive tone.

6. Sign your messages with at least your name, job title and contact number.

7. Don't use only capital letters.

8. Don't just rely on an e-mail. An e-mail can be lost. Follow-ups can often be done via the telephone or regular mail.

9. Avoid using abbreviations unless your readers are familiar with their meaning.

10. Tell people the format of any attachments you send if they're anything other than basic Microsoft Office file types.

Chapter 4
Common Writing Errors

In this chapter we point out some common writing errors that occur most frequently in the workplace by giving **real-life examples** of poor writing and showing how these might be improved.

As you proceed through the following examples, you will discover how to avoid these common writing errors at work and make your writing strong and appealing to your readers. Also, you will find comments following each example which make you aware of the writing errors and how to revise them in a better and effective way.

Remember

The key point to writing effectively is **practice**. If this is an area you really need to work hard on, I suggest you write a lot of memos and e-mails and let someone edit them to show you how you can improve them.

Example 1

Original

MEMORANDUM

To: All Employees
From: Security Manager
Date: June 4, 20xx
Subject: Company visitors' procedures

It has recently come to my attention that there are visitors to the Company who present themselves anywhere or to anyone they choose.

It is very important that all visitors check with the receptionist on the 1st Floor. The receptionist will contact the employee that the visitor has come to see, and the employee will go to the reception area to escort their visitor. There should be no unescorted visitors walking through the Company.

If you have questions, please do not hesitate to contact me.

Regards,

Hajar Jassim
Security Manager

Comments:
- Use **bullet lists** to direct attention.

MEMORANDUM

To: All Employees
From: Security Manager
Date: June 4, 20xx
Subject: Company visitors' procedures

In order to protect the company's security as well as the safety of all staff, please follow these procedures for handling visits to the main office:

- Advise visitors to report to the receptionist on the 1st Floor.
- Accompany the visitor to and from the reception and meeting area.

Your co-operation in maintaining the high level of professionalism in our office is greatly appreciated.

Regards

Hajar Jassim
Security Manager

Example 2

Original

MEMORANDUM

To: All Employees
From: Plant Manager
Date: May 15, 20xx
Subject: **New Bus Schedule**

For all employees who must travel back and forth between the airport and the production plant, we have developed a new bus schedule.

Two buses will operate beginning June 16. One bus will leave the main gate of the airport and another will leave the main gate of the production plant at 8:30 each morning. They will leave each plant every 20 minutes thereafter.

The afternoon schedule will begin at 1:20 p.m., and the last bus will leave at 4:20 p.m. Note that no buses will leave between noon and 1 p.m.

Regards,

Hajar Jassim
Plant Manager

Comments:

- Use **tables** to present numerical data in concise form and to draw the reader's attention.

To: All Employees
From: Plant Manager
Date: May 15, 20xx
Subject: **New Bus Schedule**

Whom does it concern

The new bus schedule affects all employees who must travel back and forth between the airport plant and the production plant.

Effective date

Two buses will operate beginning June 16.

Bus timings

The following table shows the bus-timing schedule for both buses leaving the main gates of each plant as follows:

Morning		Afternoon	
8:30	10:10	1:20	3:00
8:50	10:30	1:40	3:20
9:10	10:50	2:00	3:40
9:30	11:10	2:20	4:00
9:50	11:30	2:40	4:20

Note:

No buses will leave between noon and 1 p.m. and the last bus will leave at 4:20 p.m.

Regards,

Hajar Jassim
Plant Manager

Example 3

Original

MEMORANDUM

To: Project Manager
From: Electrical Engineer
Date: June 4, 20xx
Subject: Appreciation letter for Gas Project Team

Some of my colleagues have received a letter of appreciation for the above project. I was very surprised to see my name not included in the lists, as I have been contributing not only to enhance company objectives, but also to pay close attention to work being safely performed during this project.

I therefore feel very upset as my input in the abovementioned project was not considered.

This type of unfairness leads to demoralization of employees and goes against companies benchmarking in creating a healthy environment and boosting employee moral.

I am looking forward to your decision.

Regards,

Yassin Ali
Electrical Engineer

Comments:
- **Control your emotions** in business writing.

MEMORANDUM

To: Project Manager
From: Electrical Engineer
Date: June 4, 20xx
Subject: Appreciation letter for Gas Project Team

It has been noted that some employees involved in the Gas project have not been acknowledged.

Obviously, such practice is contrary to company guidelines as they relate to the employees' motivation scheme. Unfortunately, any perceived unfairness may well create an unhealthy environment among the employees.

Your reply in this matter would be much appreciated.

Regards,

Yassin Ali
Electrical Engineer

Example 4

MEMORANDUM

To: Mike Hansen
From: Mohamed Afeef
Date: June 4, 20xx
Subject: Attendance Notice

Your work has been excellent. However, your absence record is now overruling your work record. We have difficulty scheduling when we cannot depend on your attendance. We have discussed this subject with you several times before. Now your attendance must meet our requirements or we will have to issue a warning letter if we do not see immediate improvement.

Your adherence to the above is appreciated.

Mohamed Afeef
Senior Project Engineer

Comments:

- Use **short paragraphs.**
- Use **one idea per paragraph** to emphasize each important concept, so the reader will not get lost trying to understand your message.
- **Think of your reader.**

MEMORANDUM

To: Mike Hansen
From: Mohamed Afeef
Date: June 4, 20xx
Subject: Attendance Notice

This is to remind you that your absence record has affected the manpower availability and as a result your colleagues are unable to schedule their duty roster.

Therefore, you are requested to meet the operations requirements. A warning letter will be issued to you if we do not see immediate improvement.

Your adherence to the above is appreciated.

Mohamed Afeef
Senior Project Engineer

 **Example 5**

MEMORANDUM

To: All Employees
From: Transport Coordinator
Date: June 4, 20xx
Subject: Renewal of Security Pass

You are kindly requested to renew your Security Pass three months before its expiry date; this is in order to avoid any delay in obtaining it in time.

Failure to apply will be the sole responsibility of the employee. This will be a reminder for that employee whose Security Pass is expiring within three months of time.

The following necessary supporting documents are required to be submitted personally to the Transport Coordinator.

1) A duly filled security pass renewal identification form.
2) 4 sets of color passport photocopies.
3) 4 sets of security pass copies.

For any queries, please do not hesitate to contact the Transport Coordinator on 43122.

Your support, cooperation, and timely action in this respect would be much appreciated.

Important note for expatriate employees

If your <u>Residence permit</u> expires within the next three months, then you must contact the <u>Documentation Supervisor</u> (ITS No. 43122), he will assist you to complete the formalities of renewing the residence visa. Once you receive a renewed residence visa, a copy must be submitted to the RTC office.

Regards,

Ali Ahmed
Transport Coordinator

Comments:

- Use **headings** to attract your readers' attention to important information
- Use **numbers** for easy reference

Revised

MEMORANDUM

To:	All Employees
From:	Transport Coordinator
Date:	June 4, 20xx
Subject:	Renewal of Security Pass
Policy	You are kindly requested to renew your Security Pass three months before its expiry date; this is in order to avoid any delay in obtaining it in time.
Employee's responsibility	Failure to apply will be the sole responsibility of the employee. This is a reminder for employees whose Security Pass is expiring in three months time.
How to renew	Please follow the steps below to renew your security pass.

Step	Action
1	Get security passes renewal identification document from the transport office.
2	Fill in the form and attach the following: 6 recent passport size photographs (background has to be in red) 4 sets of clear passport photocopies 4 sets of clear security pass copies
3	Submit in person to the Transport coordinator

Expatriate employees — If your residence permit expires within the next three months, you must contact the Documentation Supervisor as he will assist you in completing the formalities for renewing the residence visa. Once you receive a renewed residence visa, a copy must be submitted to the transport office.

Any questions? — For any queries, please contact the Transport Coordinator on 43122

Your support and cooperation are much appreciated.
Regards,

Ali Ahmed
Transport Coordinator

Example 6

MEMORANDUM
To: Plant Manager
From: Mechanical Engineer
Date: June 4, 20xx
Subject: Salary Adjustment Request

I am writing to you to request an increase in my monthly salary. I feel this letter is necessary because I have not been offered an increase over the last five years.

I feel that I am an asset to the company. I believe I have performed all my required duties and others to the best of my ability. The skills I provide are valuable, and I'm sure you'll agree, they are an essential part of the running of this business.

I am looking forward for your approval and appreciate your comments.

Regards,

Khalid Afeef
Mechanical Engineer

Comments:
- Avoid beginning too many sentences with "**I**" in your business writing.
- Keep your paragraphs **short** and **to the point**.

MEMORANDUM

TO: Plant Manager
From: Electrical Engineer
Date: June 4, 20xx
Subject: Salary Adjustment Request

This is to request an adjustment to my monthly salary since I have not been offered an increase for the past five years.

My personal contribution toward enhancing the productivity of this department is attached for your information.

Your approval in this matter would be much appreciated.

Khalid Afeed
Electrical Engineer

 **Example 7**

To	All Employees
CC	Leadership team
Subject	Misuse of E-mail Privilege
Attachment	

We all like to send and receive e-mails, but personal mailings use up too much time and are a distraction from our work.

Therefore, all employees are requested to refrain from using their company e-mail account for personal mail. Those employees who continue to abuse their e-mail privilege will have their accounts revoked.

Remember that the account was given to you to make your job easier by facilitating quick contact with business associates, not to make it possible to communicate with family and friends.

Please respect your e-mail privilege and don't abuse it, otherwise you risk having your access to e-mail suspended.
Regards,

Ali Salem
IT Manager

Comments:
- Keep your e-mail messages **short** and **to the point**.

To	All Employees
CC	Leadership team
Subject	Misuse of E-mail Privilege
Attachment	

It has been observed that some employees have taken advantage of their company e-mail by sending non-business messages to a large group of users.

This practice is unacceptable in our environment and disciplinary action will be taken against anyone found misusing his or her e-mail.

Your co-operation would be greatly appreciated.
Regards,

Ali Salem
IT Manager

Example 8

MEMORANDUM

To: Transport Manager
From: Transport Officer
Date: October 10, 20xx
Subject: Short-term hire of buses

I'd like to tell you that we are having a bit of engine trouble with our buses at the moment and **I'm afraid** they'll almost definitely be off the road for a week or so. What I want to say is quite a problem for us because **I'll** need the buses next Wednesday.

So, **I think** the best way to get round this problem is for us to hire the same sort of bus for the time being just until our mechanics can get our buses back on the road.

Can you tell me if you think this idea is **OK**?

Ivan Naser
Transport Officer

Comments:

- The language used in the above memo is appropriate spoken English.
- Do not use **contractions**.
  Contractions are the words formed from two abbreviated words, such as "I'd", "I'm" and "they'll." Write the words in full.
- Do not use **informal expressions** such as "I think," "I'm afraid," "what I want to say" and "ok."

MEMORANDUM

To: Transport Manager
From: Transport Officer
Date: October 10, 20xx
Subject: Short-term hire of buses

Both buses used to transport passengers between the company head office and the fields are currently under repair due to engine problems. They are likely to be out of service for at least a week.

Therefore, it is recommended that two similar buses be hired temporarily until our vehicles are roadworthy again.

Your approval would be appreciated.

Ivan Naser
Transport Officer

 **Example 9**

To	requests@abc.com
CC	
Subject	Car Loan Request
Attachment	Car Loan Application Form

Please find attached herewith the car loan application form **pursuant to your request**.

Please complete the attached form and **forward to the undersigned latest by July 10, 20xx** in order to complete the processing formalities.
Regards,

Mohamed Hamdi
Human Resources Coordinator

Comments:

Remove the **old-fashioned phrases** in the above e-mail message as illustrated below:

- "**Please find attached herewith**" is an old-fashioned phrase and can be replaced by "**Attached is.**"
- "**Pursuant to your request**" can be replaced by "**As requested.**"
- "**Forward to the undersigned**" can be replaced by "**Send it to me.**"

To   requests@abc.com

CC

Subject   Car loan request

Attachment   Car loan application form

Attached is the car loan application form as requested.

Pleases complete the attached form and send it to me before July 10, 20xx.

Regards,

Mohamed Hamdi

Human Resources Coordinator

 **Example 10**

Original

To:　　　　mhamad@abc.com
CC:
Subject:　　English Language Training Proposal

Dear Hamad,

As requested, I have attached a proposal **4** your employees **2** come & study business communication @ Zayed University.

I will get in touch with you shortly **2** discuss about your requirements for a custom programme.
Regards,

Hajar Khaled
Training Coordinator

Comments:

• Avoid using SMS language in your business e-mails.

To: mhamad@abc.com
CC:
Subject: English Language Training Proposal

Dear Hamad,

As requested, I have attached a proposal for your employees to come and study business communication at Zayed University.

I will get in touch with you shortly to discuss about your requirements for a custom programme.
Regards,

Hajar Khaled
Training Coordinator

Chapter 5
Useful Business Phrases

This chapter provides you with the most common business phrases that are often used in business correspondence. These phrases are divided into sections according to their purpose. The idea is that you can copy them directly into your day-to-day business correspondence.

Common business phrases

1. Referring to a previous communication

2. Requests

3. Referring to a negative issue

4. Enclosing documents

5. Condolences

6. Congratulations

7. Apologies

8. Recommendations

9. Closing phrases

1. Referring to a previous communication

- **With reference to your** [fax / memo / e-mail] **dated** [ ] **regarding** ...
- **I/We refer to your** [fax / memo / e-mail] **dated** [ ] **regarding** ...
- **Further to** our [telephone conversation /discussions], this is to inform you that ...
- **With reference to** your [fax / memo / e-mail] **dated** [ ], we are glad to inform you that ...

Below are five examples on how to use the above business phrases:

Example 1

With reference to your e-mail dated January 24, 20xx please find attached our comments regarding last week's development seminar.

Example 2

We refer to your comments regarding the fire extinguishers which were raised by the safety team after the last safety inspection. I am pleased to report that all fire extinguishers have been re-positioned and are now easier to access in case of fire.

Example 3

Further to our telephone conversation today, I would like to confirm that your order will be delivered on May 13, 20xx. Please contact us again if you require any information.

Example 4

Further to our discussions, please be informed that the audit meeting will be held on Wednesday, November 4, 20xx, at 10 a.m. in the conference room.

Your attendance will be highly appreciated.

Example 5

With reference to our fax dated March 15, 20xx, we are still waiting to hear from you concerning employee workshops for stress management.

We will appreciate your reply by March 25, 20xx.

Example 6

With reference to your e-mail dated January 24, 20xx regarding your proposal on the Risk Assessment training program, we are glad to inform you that your proposal met our requirement.

2. Requests

- **It would be appreciated if you could** . . .
- **Please** . . .
- **You are (kindly) requested to** . . .
- **I would appreciate** . . .

Below are four examples of how to use the above business phrases:

Example 1

It would be appreciated if you could approve my request to attend the Gitex Exhibition for two days.

Example 2

Please submit a copy of your driver's license to the transport office before March 15, 20xx.

Example 3

You are kindly requested to review the attached documents regarding the power upgrade project and to let me have your comments before May 15, 20xx.

Example 4

I would appreciate receiving a copy of the financial report by July 15, 20xx.

3. Referring to a negative issue

- It has come to my [attention/notice] that . . .
- It has been [observed/noticed] that . . .
- I /We have [noticed/observed] that . . .

Below are four examples on how to use the above business phrases:

Example 1

It has come to my notice that some employees residing in the non-smoking wings smoke in their rooms. This practice is against the company's non-smoking policy.

Therefore, residents in the non-smoking wings are requested to stop smoking.

Your adherence to company policy is appreciated.

Example 2

It has been noticed that some employees are removing their office furniture to the new Administration building.

You are therefore requested to return all removed furniture immediately and hand over the old furniture to the services coordinator, Mr. Ali.

Example 3

It has been observed that some employees are sending non-business related e-mails to a large number of employees.

This is to remind everyone that e-mail is a communication tool and should only be used for business related communication.

Those who wish to share other information of value and interest to some employees can use the discussion forum which is available in our company intranet.

Example 4

We have noticed that some employees are using their mobile phones with camera facility in the oil field area, which is contrary to management instructions.

Therefore, all heads of departments are urgently requested to remind their staff to avoid using mobile phones with camera facilities.

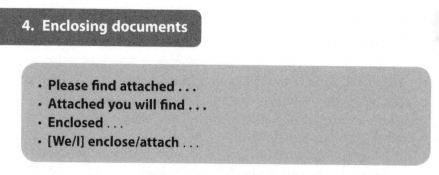

4. Enclosing documents

- **Please find attached . . .**
- **Attached you will find . . .**
- **Enclosed . . .**
- **[We/I] enclose/attach . . .**

Below are four examples on how to use the above business phrases:

Example 1

Please find attached a copy of the safety training matrix.

Example 2

Attached you will find a copy of the safety training matrix.

Example 3

Enclosed is a copy of the safety training matrix for your information.

Example 4

We attach the updated listing of the new safety video tapes available on the training.

5. Condolences

- **With deep sorrow, this is to announce the sad demise of the** [father/mother/wife/son/daughter] of [name]. May God bless his soul in peace. We express our heartfelt condolences to Mr./Ms. [name] and his family.
- **It is with profound sorrow, that we announce the sad demise of our colleague**, [name], [job title] on [date]. We express our heartfelt condolences to the bereaved family.
- **It is with deep regret and sorrow, that we convey the sad demise of the** [brother/sister/mother/father/wife/son/daughter] of Mr./Ms. [name]. We pray for the almighty Allah to give the bereaved family the courage and strength to bear this great loss.

Below are two examples of how to use the above business phrases:

Example 1

With deep sorrow, this is to announce the sad demise of the father of Mr. Hassan.

We truly hope that Hassan and his family can gather the strength and courage during this difficult time.

Example 2

With deep sorrow, we regret to inform you of the sad demise of the mother of Mr. Ahmed today in Lebanon. May God give him and his family the courage and strength to bear this severe loss, and may the departed soul rest in peace.

On behalf of ABC Management, we express our heartfelt condolences to the bereaved family.

6. Congratulations

> - **Congratulations on . . .**
> - **On behalf of . . . , I congratulate you on . . .**
> - **We congratulate you on . . .**
> - **Please accept my congratulations on . . .**

Below are four examples of how to use the above phrases in a business context:

Example 1

Congratulations on your promotion to Supervisor.

This promotion is in recognition of the excellent work you have done for this company.

We are very confident that you will meet the new responsibilities which accompany the position of Supervisor with the same level of enthusiasm which you have demonstrated.

Example 2

I am pleased to advise that with effect from June 1, 20xx, Mr. Khaled Al Maskari has been appointed IT Manager of ABC.

This position, as we all know, is a very important position in our organization, we therefore request your full support for Khaled and his team.

On behalf of ABC Management, we congratulate Khaled on his new assignment and wish him every success.

Example 3

We congratulate you on your recent promotion to Operations Manager at ABC Company. This new position will present opportunities that will challenge your experience of the past 10 years in the field.

We hope you will continue to keep ABC Company an integral part of your plans for growth. Best wishes for a successful future as Operations Manager.

Example 4

It was with great pleasure that I read of your promotion to the position of [position] with [name of firm]!

I am sure your firm has made a very wise choice and that you will excel in your new role as [position].

Please accept my congratulations on your promotion and my very best wishes for your continued success.

7. Apologies

- We are sorry to inform you that . . .
- Due to circumstances beyond our control we are sorry to inform you that . . .
- Please accept my apologies for the . . .
- We apologize for . . .
- We are sorry for any inconvenience.

Below are six examples of how to use the above business phrases:

 Example 1

We are sorry to inform you that we are unable to make delivery on the above referenced purchase order on the date indicated.

Please accept our apologies for this delay and thank you for your understanding.

 Example 2

Due to changes and events beyond our control, we will post-pone our meeting for this week and meet next Monday, February 20, 20xx at the conference room.

Please accept our apologies for any inconvenience this has caused you.

 Example 3

Please accept my apologies for missing the safety meeting on December 15, 20xx.

I had planned on attending this meeting but my wife had an emergency.

Example 4

We apologize for the way you were treated by our accounting department.

Under no circumstances should a customer be shown anything but excellent service.

Thank you for bringing this problem to our attention and we are taking steps to avoid this kind of behavior in the future.

Example 5

This is to inform you that the Airport road will be closed for one week to construct road humps starting from May 4, 20xx.

Appropriate signboards and flashlights will be made available during the above period to alert the drivers.

We apologize for any inconvenience and thank you for your patience.

Example 6

Please be informed that the afternoon clinic on Tuesday, June 7, 20xx will be closed at 8:00 p.m. (instead of 9:00 p.m.) for operational reasons.

The duty doctor will be on-call for any emergencies.

We are sorry for any inconvenience.

8. Recommendations

- **It is [recommended/suggested/proposed] that** specifications should be changed.
- **I would like to [recommend/suggest/propose] that** we should change the specification.
- **I would like to [recommend/suggest/propose]** changing the specifications.

Below are two examples on how to use the above business phrases:

Example 1

This is to inform you that the booking for indoor cycling at the ABC club has significantly increased. As a result, many members were unable to use this equipment.

Therefore, **it is recommended** that extra machines be brought in to fulfill all members' needs.

Example 2

This is to inform you that the booking for indoor cycling at the ABC club has significantly increased. As a result, many members were unable to use this equipment.

I therefore recommend bringing extra machines to fulfill all members' needs.

9. Closing phrases

- Your co-operation in this matter would be greatly appreciated.
- Your [co-operation/support] would be appreciated.
- Your support would be greatly appreciated.
- Your reply by . . . would be appreciated.
- Please [contact/call] me if [you have any questions/you require any information]
- [I/We] would appreciate your [comments/reply/feedback] on this matter by . . .
- Your adherence to the above is appreciated.
- I look forward to receiving your approval on this matter.

Here are nine examples on how to use the above business phrases:

Example 1

It has been noticed that some employees are removing their office furniture to the new Administration building.

You are therefore requested to return all removed furniture immediately and hand over the old furniture to the services coordinator, Mr. Ali.

Your co-operation in this matter would be greatly appreciated.

Example 2

I have recently noticed that it is becoming increasingly difficult to maintain cleanliness and order in the supply room.

It is everyone's responsibility to keep the supply room neat and tidy.

Your co-operation would be appreciated.

Example 3

Please be informed that our supervisor Mr. Khalid is involved in many activities. Since he is so busy, I would like to suggest that you handle the power upgrade project.

Your support would be greatly appreciated.

Example 4

Please send us more information concerning your direct deposit option as well as the monthly paperwork required to release funds for direct deposit.

Your reply by May 15, 20xx would be appreciated.

Example 5

Attached is the outline of an upcoming course on Health and Safety which will be held from March 27–31, 20xx in Dubai.

Please contact me if you have any questions.

Example 6

This is to remind you that your annual performance review is due next month. I have scheduled a review meeting with you in my office at 11a.m. on Monday, February 15, 20xx.

Please call me to confirm whether you can attend the meeting at the above time and date.

Example 7

I have received a personal invitation to attend the Power Generation Exhibition which will be held from 19th till 21st May 20xx at the Dubai International Exhibition Center.

I would appreciate your approval to attend this exhibition.

Example 8

This is to remind you that your absence record has affected the manpower availability and as a result your colleagues are unable to schedule their duty roster.

Therefore, you are requested to meet the operations requirements. A warning letter will be issued to you if we do not see immediate improvement.

Your adherence to the above is appreciated.

Example 9

This is to inform you that a career development conference will be held on May 15–20, 20xx at the Sheraton Hotel.

The conference would certainly enhance my knowledge and allow me to exchange practical ideas with the participants. Therefore, it would be appreciated if I could attend this conference.

I look forward to receiving your approval on this matter.

Chapter 6
Avoid Confusing Words

This chapter highlights words that are most commonly misused in everyday writing tasks, and gives contextual examples to help the writer appreciate the difference.

Here is a list of these easily confused words, along with their actual meaning and examples of their correct usage.

Accept	Except
Accept means "to receive."	**Except** means "not including."
Please **accept** my gift.	We found everything **except** the right document.
Access	**Excess**
Access means "admittance, a way of approach."	**Excess** means "larger amount than needed."
No one had **access** to the office.	The contract was in **excess** of $1 million.
Advice	**Advise**
Advice (noun): is an "opinion about what should be done."	**Advise** (verb): means "to recommend."
The instructor gave good **advice**.	The officer **advised** the driver to slow down.
Affect	**Effect**
Affect is usually a verb meaning "to influence."	**Effect** is usually a noun meaning "result."
The cost will **affect** the final contract.	His opinion had no **effect** on my decision.

Believe	Belief
Believe (verb)	**Belief** (noun)
I **believe** a bonus for our employees should be based on employees' performance.	I have been informed that two employees at the ABC branch do not eat certain meats due to their religious **beliefs**.

Complement	Compliment
Complement means "to complete something."	**Compliment** means "praise" or "congratulate."
That blue tie **complements** the grey shirt.	Mr. Ali **complimented** us on our efficient office.

Co-operation	Corporation
Co-operation means working together.	**Corporation** is a business organization.
Please extend our thanks to your employees for their **co-operation**.	Our computer software **corporation** is interested in finding unique Web site designers.

Farther	Further
Use **"farther"** to refer to physical distance.	Use **"further"** to mean additional.
The new office supply store is **farther** from our office than we expected.	Ali will provide **further** information about the workstation at the next meeting.

Insure	Ensure
Insure means "to protect with insurance."	**Ensure** means "to make certain."
I **insured** my house against theft for $10,000.	The operator must **ensure** that valves A and B are never open at the same time.

Moral	Morale
Moral refers to ethical belief.	**Morale** means spirit.
Khalid's strong **moral** sense prevented him from cheating.	The **morale** of the employees has increased since they received a bonus.

Patience	Patients
Patience: self-control, endurance	**Patients**: sick people
He has no **patience** with small children.	The doctor must visit his **patients** at the hospital.

Personal	Personnel
Use **"personal"** when discussing something relating to a particular person.	Use **"personnel"** to discuss the staff of an organization.
Leave your **personal** belongings over there.	The **personnel** department has your salary record.

Practice	Practise
Practice is the noun (British English).	**Practise** is the verb.
The **practice** has been cancelled.	He must **practise** every day.

Precede	Proceed
Precede means "to come before."	**Proceed** means "to go forward."
We knew that the keynote speaker **preceded** the speaker we wanted to hear.	We decided to **proceed** with the project.

Stationary	Stationery
Stationary (adjective): having a fixed place	**Stationery** (noun) refers to office supplies.
A security guard stands in a **stationary** position.	Could you go to the store and get me some **stationery.**

Weather	Whether
Weather: the temperature or conditions outside.	**Whether**: used when talking about a choice between two possibilities.
The trip was cancelled due to bad **weather**.	I am writing to find out **whether** you have rooms available in the Sheraton Hotel in the second week of May.

Chapter 7
Personal Business Documents

This chapter covers the most common personal letters that you can familiarize yourself with for your own correspondence needs. These letters have been divided into three categories:

- Employee's request letters
- Congratulation letters
- Appreciation letters

1. Employee request

 Course or conference request (sample 1)

To:
From:
Date:
Subject: **Report Writing Course**

As part of my career development, I am interested in attending the above mentioned course, which will be held in [Location], from [Date] to [Date].

This course will certainly enhance my knowledge, and enable me to gain practical skills that will be valuable in my field.

Your support would be greatly appreciated.
Regards,

[Name]
[Job Title]

Course or conference request (sample 2)

> To:
> From:
> Date:
> Subject: **Career Development Conference**
>
> This is to inform you that a Career Development Conference will be held on (Date) in (Location) at the (Location).
>
> The conference would certainly enhance my knowledge and allow me to exchange practical ideas with the participants.
>
> Therefore, it would be appreciated if I could attend this conference.
> Regards,
>
> [Name]
> [Job Title]

Car loan request

> To:
> From:
> Date:
> Subject: **Car Loan Request**
>
> This is to inform you that I am currently employed as a (Job Title) since (Date).
>
> It would be appreciated if you could consider my request for a car loan in order to avoid bank interest rates.
>
> Your support would be appreciated.
> Regards,
>
> [Name]
> [Job Title]

Leaving due to illness

To:
From:
Date:
Subject: **Leaving due to illness**

As you know, I have been very unwell for some time now and, as a consequence, feel that I am unable to work for (Name of Company) any longer.

This was not an easy decision and took a lot of consideration. However, please be assured that I will do all I can to assist in the smooth transfer of my responsibilities before leaving.

I wish both you and (Name of Company) every good fortune and I would like to thank you for having me as part of your team.
Regards,

[Name]
[Job Title]

Moving to another company

To:
From:
Date:
Subject: **Moving to another company**

I have decided that it is time to move on and I have accepted a position elsewhere. This was not an easy decision and took a lot of consideration. However, I am confident that my new role will help me to achieve some of the goals I have for my career.

Please be assured that I will do all I can to assist in the smooth transfer of my responsibilities before leaving.

I wish both you and (Name of Company) every good fortune and I would like to thank you for having me as part of your team.
Regards,

[Name]
[Job Title]

Mobile phone request

To:
From:
Date:
Subject: **Mobile Phone Request**

This is to draw to your attention that my job requirements dictate that I use my personal mobile for business communication.

I seek your support to provide me with a mobile phone as per the company policy.

Regards,

[Name]
[Job Title]

Patient accompany request

To:
From:
Date:
Subject: **Patient Accompany Request**

This is to inform you that my (father) has been hospitalized in the (Name) Hospital

My (father's) treatment will be carried out overseas and it could take a few months until recovery.

Therefore, I am seeking your support and approval to accompany my (father) to help (him) as indicated in the medical report (see attached).

Regards,

[Name]
[Job Title]

Resignation letter (sample 1)

To:
From:
Date:
Subject: **Resignation**

This is to inform you that I have decided to go back to my country due to personal problems.

I have worked with (Name of Company) since (Date) and it has been a pleasure working for (Name of Company). I feel it is time to look for further challenges in addition to being with the family.

Please accept my resignation as (Job Title), effective from (Date).

Thank you for the rewarding experience I have enjoyed during my (seven-year) association with the organization.
Regards,

[Name]
[Job Title]

Resignation letter (sample 2)

To:
From:
Date:
Subject: **Resignation**

As required by my contract of employment, I give you (four weeks) notice of my intention to leave my position as (Job Title).

I wish both you and (Name of Company) every good fortune and I would like to thank you for having me as part of your team.
Regards,

[Name]
[Job Title]

Resignation letter (sample 3)

To:
From:
Date:
Subject: **Resignation**

It is with deep regret that after (eight) years with (Name of Company), I must resign my position, effective (Date).

Financial considerations, and family obligations, require that I accept a position that demands less travel and time spent away from home.

The opportunity for growth and continuing challenges offered by (Name of Company) in these past (eight) years have been of great personal and professional value to me. I will miss the personal closeness and the consideration shown by all members of the company.
Regards,

[Name]
[Job Title]

Resignation letter (sample 4)

To:
From:
Date:
Subject: **Resignation**

I have accepted a position as (New Job Position) at (Name of Company). I am looking forward to my new position and the challenges that await me.

Please accept my resignation as (Job Title), effective (Date).

I appreciate having had the opportunity to work for such a fine company. I wish you and the organization continued success.
Regards,

[Name]
[Job Title]

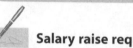

Salary raise request (sample 1)

To:
From:
Date:
Subject: **Salary Raise Request**

This is to request an **adjustment** in my monthly salary since I have not been offered an increase over the last (five) years.

I have performed all my required duties to the best of my ability and the skills I provide are an essential part of (Mechanical) section.

Your consideration and approval in this matter would be greatly appreciated.
Regards,

[Name]
[Job Title]

Salary raise request (sample 2)

To:
From:
Date:
Subject: **Salary Raise Request**

I appreciate the opportunity I have had during the past (three) years of serving as (Job Title). This past year has been an especially challenging business environment, and I have every hope that the success achieved will continue for the near future.

Here is a list of my most signification contributions to the department and the company in the past three years:

- . . . .
- . . . .

I am confident that you will offer a salary increase that reflects my input and my standing in the department.
Regards,

[Name]
[Job Title]

Study leave request (sample 1)

To:
From:
Date:
Subject: **Study Leave Request**

This is to inform you that I have been accepted for a one year program scholarship from (Name of Company) to get a Master's degree in (Business Administration).

Therefore, I would appreciate if you could allow me to take a study leave with pay or with half pay for the abovementioned period to support my family during my absence while on study leave.

Your consideration and support in this matter would be greatly appreciated.
Regards,

[Name]
[Job Title]

Study leave request (sample 2)

To:
From:
Date:
Subject: **Study leave Request**

This is to bring to your attention that I wish to complete my studies at the (Name of the College). This will help me achieve some of the goals I have for my career and benefit (Name of Company) in return.

Your support in granting me study leave would be greatly appreciated.
Regards,

[Name]
[Job Title]

Study leave request (sample 3)

To:
From:
Date:
Subject: **Study Leave Request**

After completion of (six) years in (ABC), I feel that I need to move forward to further continue my education at (Name of College).

I am sure that (ABC) management team is committed to enhance the potential of UAE Nationals to develop their skills in order to meet (ABC) business needs.

Therefore, I would greatly appreciate it if you would consider my request favorably and assist my career development.
Regards,

[Name]
[Job Title]

Transfer request

To:
From:
Date:
Subject: **Transfer Request to the Main Office**

This is to draw your attention to the fact that my (mother's) health condition is getting worse which is affecting my family life and my career as well.

I would appreciate your understanding and support for my request to transfer me to the main office.
Regards,

[Name]
[Job Title]

2. Congratulations

Promotion (sample 1)

To:
From:
Date:
Subject: Promotion

Congratulations on your promotion to (Job Title). I know how hard you have worked to earn the recognition you presently enjoy at (Name of Company), and I feel that they have made a very wise choice.

Please accept our best wishes for your success in your new position.

[Name]
[Job Title]

Promotion (sample 2)

To:
From:
Date:
Subject: Promotion

It was with great pleasure that I read of your promotion to the position of (Job Title) with (Name of Company). I am sure your firm has made a very wise choice and that you will excel in your new role as (Job Title).

Please accept my congratulations on your promotion and my very best wishes for your continued success.

[Name]
[Job Title]

3. Appreciation

Appreciation (sample 1)

To:
From:
Date:
Subject: Appreciation

I appreciated your prompt time-keeping and excellent perform-ance during your training period.

We are delighted to congratulate you on having set an example to many others during your training period and we recognize your dedication and commitment.

I hope that you will continue to maintain a good performance record and wish you all the success in completing your training period.
Regards

[Name]
[Job Title]

Appreciation (sample 2)

To:
From:
Date:
Subject: Appreciation

I would like to convey my sincere appreciation to you for handing over the Lost & Found money in the pool car on (Date) to the appropriate department.

Your honesty is remarkable. It sets a fine example to others and also highlights the duty of the individual.

We applaud your honesty and convey the gratitude of the owner.

[Name]
[Job Title]

Appreciation (sample 3)

To:
From:
Date:
Subject: Appreciation

I would like to take this opportunity to convey our great appreciation for your dedication to your work during the last (. . .) years.

You play a vital role in our operations to maintain a safe working environment.

We trust that you will continue to provide such excellent service in the future.
Regards

[Name]
[Job Title]

Appreciation (sample 4)

To:
From:
Date:
Subject: Appreciation

We are pleased to note your keen interest and active participation during the final commissioning phase of the (Name of Project)

Your dedication and enthusiasm to learn are indeed noteworthy.

We would take this opportunity to convey our appreciation for your dedication and look forward to your continued progress in the future.
Regards

[Name]
[Job Title]

Appreciation (sample 5)

To:
From:
Date:
Subject: Appreciation

I am pleased to advise you that your attendance and training records reveal prompt time-keeping, excellent performance and consistent progress.

I would like to take this opportunity to convey our appreciation of your dedication to your work and of your compliance with company policies.

We hope that you will continue to maintain this good practice to accomplish your training period successfully and set an example to many new entrants.
Regards,

[Name]
[Job Title]

Appreciation (sample 6)

To:
From:
Date:
Subject: Appreciation

It gives me great pleasure to note your outstanding efforts for (. . . .) in a safe and professional manner.

I would like to take this opportunity to congratulate you on your hard work and hope that you will keep up the same spirit in order to deal with future challenges.
Regards,

[Name]
[Job Title]

Appreciation (sample 7)

To:
From:
Date:
Subject: Appreciation

I have great pleasure in acknowledging your contribution during the overhaul activities of (Project name).

Your motivation, dedication and safety awareness will definitely contribute to accomplishing our objectives on schedule.

I would like to take this opportunity to convey our appreciation of your initiative and hope that you will keep up your dedication and hard work.
Regards,

[Name]
[Job Title]

Appreciation (sample 8)

To:
From:
Date:
Subject: Appreciation

This letter is to acknowledge the effort made and assistance you have given to make the safety campaign a successful and recognized event.

I would like to take this opportunity to express the management's appreciation and to wish you every success in future events.
Regards,

[Name]
[Job Title]

References

Angel, David, and Brent Heslop, *The Elements of E-mail Style*. Reading, MA: Addison Wesley (1994)

Bailey, E.P., *Plain English at Work*. New York: Oxford University Press (1996)

Bartram, Peter, *Perfect Business Writing*. London: Arrow Business Books (1993)

Beer, David, and David McMurrey, *A Guide to Writing as an Engineer*. NJ: John Wiley & Sons (1997)

Bernhardt, Stephen, and Edward L. Smith, *Writing at Work: Professional Skills for People on the Job*. Lincolnwood, IL: NTC (1997)

Billingham, Jo, *Editing and Revising Text*. Oxford: Oxford University Press (1998)

Bond, Alan, *Over 300 Successful Business Letters for All Occasions*. NY: Barron's Educational Series (1998)

Brown, Ralph, *Making Business Writing Happen: A Simple and Effective Guide to Writing Well*. Allen & Unwin (2003)

Chesla, Elizabeth, *Improving Your Writing for Work*, Second Edition. New York: Learning Express (2000)

Dobson, Ann, *How to Write Business Letters*. Delhi: Jaico Publishing House (2002)

Doherty, Michael, and Susan Swift, *Write for Business: Skills for Effective Report Writing*. London: Longman (1992)

Doherty, Michael, *Writing for Excellence: Four-Stage Approach to Creating Maximum Impact in Business Writing*. New York: McGraw-Hill (1992)

Dugger, Jim, *Business Letters for Busy People*. National Press Publications (2002)

Fielding, Michael, *Effective Communication in Organisations: Preparing Messages That Communicate*. Second Edition. Cape Town: Juta (1997)

Finkelstein, L., Jr., *Pocket Book of Technical Writing for Engineers and Scientists*. New York: McGraw-Hill (2000)

Fruehling, Rosemary and N.B. Oldham, *Write to the Point*. New York: McGraw-Hill (1998)

Gentle, Robert, *Business Writing that Works*, Upper Saddle River, NJ: Prentice Hall (2002)

Guffey, Mary Ellen, *Business Communication: Process and Product*. Third Edition. South-Western (2000)

Guffey, Mary, *Essentials of Business Communication*. Fifth Edition. South-Western/Cengage Learning (2001)

Heritage, Katharine, *Report Writing in a Week*. London: Hodder & Stoughton (2003)

Huth, E.J., *Writing and Publishing in Medicine*. Third Edition. Baltimore: Williams & Wilkins (1999)

Iacone, Salvatore, *Write to the Point: How to Communicate in Business with Style and Purpose*. Franklin Lakes, NJ: Career Press (2003)

Jones, D., *The Technical Communicator's Handbook*. Needham Heights, MA: Allyn & Bacon (2000)

Langosch, Sydney L., *Writing American Style*. Barron's Educational Series (1999)

Lunsford, Andrea, and Robert Cannors, *The Everyday Writer: A Brief Reference*. New York: St. Martin's Press (1998)

Munter, Mary, *Guide to Managerial Communication*. Sixth Edition. Upper Saddle River, NJ: Prentice Hall (2002)

Pearsall, T., *The Elements of Technical Writing*. Needham Heights, MA: Allyn and Bacon (2001)

Riordan, Daniel G. and Steven E. Pauley, *Technical Report Writing Today*. Eighth Edition. Boston and New York: Houghton Miffin (2002)

Seely, John, *Writing Reports*. Oxford: Oxford University Press (2002)

Sparks, Suzanne D., *The Manager's Guide to Business Writing*. New York: McGraw-Hill (1999)

Strunk, William, and E.B. White, *The Elements of Style*. Needham Heights: Allyn & Bacon (2000)

Taylor, Shirley, *Guide to Effective E-mails*. Singapore: Trans Quest Asia Publishers (2001)

Taylor, Shirley, *Model Business Letters, E-mails and Other Business Documents*. Sixth Edition. Upper Saddle River, NJ: Prentice Hall (2004)

Trimble, John R., *Writing with Style: Conversations on the Art of Writing*. Second Edition. Upper Saddle River, NJ: Prentice Hall (2000)

Vanalstyne, J. and M. Tritt, *Professional and Technical Writing Strategies*. Upper Saddle River, NJ: Prentice Hall (2002)

Watson, Jane, *Business Writing Basics*. Second Edition. Vancouver: Self-Counsel Press (2002)

Williams, Joseph, *Style: Ten Lessons in Clarity and Grace*. Sixth Edition. New York, Addison, Wesley & Longman (2001)

Acknowledgements

I would like to thank Dr. Clarence Emslie, Senior English Language Teacher working for Saudi Development and Training in the Kingdom of Saudi Arabia for encouraging me to write this book and I do appreciate his valuable input and feedback.

I also thank Michael Doherty, Director of Professional Communication Services in the United Kingdom for his valuable input and recommendations.

Many thanks to Peter Hardcastle, Curriculum and Assessment Advisor in ADNOC Technical Institute (ATI) in Abu Dhabi, United Arab Emirates for his constructive feedback.

I am grateful to the many colleagues at work for their feedback without which this book would not have been in its present shape.

Finally, I thank my family for their love, understanding and support during the process of writing this book.

Index